Life-Cha

MAXIMS *of*
LIFE & BUSINESS
With Selected Prayers

**Executive
Books**

Life-Changing Classics, Volume VII

MAXIMS *of*
LIFE & BUSINESS
With Selected Prayers

Published by
Executive Books
206 West Allen Street
Mechanicsburg, PA 17055
717-766-9499   800-233-2665
Fax: 717-766-6565
www.ExecutiveBooks.com

ISBN: 0-937539-80-5

United in the United States of America

TABLE OF CONTENTS

FOREWORD

THE introduction of the one-price system, first inaugurated by John Wanamaker in the year 1865, has been a leaven in the business world that has worked its beneficent influence everywhere. Honesty as a business asset is now fully recognized. If the goods are cotton and look like wool, you are frankly told that the article may be a yard wide but it is not all wool. Only a few years ago if you wanted a pair of trousers you took a day off and negotiated for them. Clothing merchants, as a class, used to take us in and do for us, being strangers, throwing in a pair of suspenders, and a box of paper collars as a salve for a bad bargain. Now the wisdom of the rule of absolute frankness is universally recognized.

The one-price system, as opposed to the Oriental plan of haggle, and the customs of the booth and bazaar, is a saver of nerve-force beyond computation. Why should men seek to overreach one another? And the answer is: There is no reason. The way to succeed is to keep faith with your customer and secure him as a friend. We make our money out of our friends; our enemies will not do business with us. So the concern that has the most friends does the most business. And that is why the Wanamaker Stores set the retailers of the world a pace—their customers are their friends and their friends are their customers.—**From "The Age of Commonsense," a lecture by Elbert Hubbard.**

Biography of
JOHN WANAMAKER

Born in Philadelphia on July 11, 1838, John Wanamaker created the first department store and later became famous as a merchant for his upscale clothing stores and department stores on the East Coast. He first opened his small men's store in his home town of Philadelphia in 1861, but was one of America's largest merchants by the early 1900s. His innovative sales and marketing strategies attracted customers like a magnet and set his business apart as the hub of center city Philadelphia.

With a philosophy that extended beyond merely running a business for personal profit, Wanamaker viewed his business as a vital means of positively impacting the prosperity of an entire city and the nation at large for the betterment of all.

He was a powerful and innovative businessman who undoubtedly helped various inner cities and urban communities to thrive with great success during his day and time. He supported a 3,000-member church which ran a library, school, savings bank, and employment service. He also supported a number of other religious organizations and recruited many of his employees from them as well. He provided jobs for 15,000 people in Philadelphia and New York. He also provided opportunities for blacks and women to work in business during a time when it was common to exclude them. He was also actively involved in politics and held the position of U. S. Postmaster General while President Benjamin

Harrison was in office. John Wanamaker's other contributions included the construction of a hospital, a museum, and a temporary housing shelter for men who fell on hard times. Aside from being an extraordinary businessman, he was a great humanitarian with a passion for helping the less fortunate.

Also recognized for his upstanding principles, Wanamaker stood for truth in advertising as well as "Accuracy in Word and Print." Wanamaker retail policies have been credited as key factors in the rise of department store ethics and procedures. And his devout commitment to his Christian faith along with his support of various religious and patriotic causes also made him a renowned pillar of the community.

Back in 1899, the legendary merchant was worth $25 million and his stores had higher sales figures than any other retailer in the world. He had two stores in Philadelphia and New York and was selling more than $15 million worth of merchandise each year. Because John Wanamaker primarily viewed his business as a service to the community, he inspired countless thousands to have a love affair with the department store concept.

He also possessed a powerfully creative imagination that attracted consumers to his stores like P.T. Barnum attracted kids to the circus. Wanamaker was innovative in terms of introducing unique marketing strategies that consisted of aggressive advertising, white sales, money-back guarantees, newspaper ads, the world's largest organ, free entertainment, pageants, and a restaurant inside the store. His department stores showcased electric lights, moving-pictures, moving stairs (at a time when escalators were unheard of), airplanes, and automobiles. Just as some of the Wanamaker Department Store ads implied, many of the dazzled customers of this great era believed that "A tour through Wanamaker's is a tour 'round the world." The next time you take a journey through a department store, think about John Wanamaker—the "Merchant Prince" who was the originator of the department store concept.

At 8 a.m. on December 12, 1922, John Wanamaker died at the age of 84. He left more than $40 million to his heirs. His funeral held on December 14 at the Bethany Church attracted 15,000 people. The church could only seat 2,500 and most of the mourners stood outside in the snow. The large crowd of mourners was a testament to a compassionate Christian businessman who had made an enormous contribution to his city. With 175 honorary pallbearers representing numerous ethnic and religious groups in Philadelphia, Wanamaker's funeral was such as might be held for a President of the United States. The City Council suspended many of the operations in the city and Senator George Wharton Pepper summed up the beloved John Wanamaker's contribution to the City of Brotherly Love: "Mr. Wanamaker has enriched Philadelphia materially and spiritually. His wonderful store stands as a monument to his power to imagine great results and then make them a reality. His commercial life is an example of an unwavering service to his community."

Our Best Friend Is the One Who Helps Us to Find Out Our Real

selves and who endeavors to show us how to make proper use of our abilities.

A school or college teacher who sees no other duty in her position than cramming heads with book knowledge alone is next door to a failure.

To help make the coming man somebody must study the headpiece and the heartpiece of every individual under his care and aid him to sift his book knowledge and apply to himself the part that will develop the plans of his life.

If he has no plans for his life, lose no time in helping him to find himself.

Let us be practical in keeping store and in everything else we have to do.

[Signed] *John Wanamaker*

Oct. 26, 1920.

One of more than 5,000 newspaper editorials written by John Wanamaker

WHEN a great and good life goes out after a continual influence for the uplift of mankind through many years, the loss is startling and sometimes appalling. At such a time it is very important to continue that inspiring influence as powerfully and strongly as is possible. It is a clear duty to mankind.

A friend, who was long the most intimate associate of Mr. Wanamaker, has felt it to be his duty to preserve, in convenient form, these sayings of Mr. Wanamaker, and in so doing he has made us all his debtors.

This painstaking task has not been performed as a cold duty, but is dictated by a warm and deep friendship which Mr. Wanamaker appreciated greatly. Therefore, these wise sayings, which speak for themselves, mean much more, as they so clearly and forcibly represent the tribute of a large-hearted friend. In this unique collection Mr. Wanamaker's precious influence will be extended through the many years to come.

The assistance of Mr. Gordon H. Cilley has been very important, and is gratefully acknowledged.

RUSSELL H. CONWELL
February 15, 1923

WANAGRAMS:
MAXIMS OF LIFE & BUSINESS

BUSINESS AND SUCCESS

Taking good care of a small sum, saved week by week, has been in thousands of cases the foundation of a large fortune.

It is not extraordinary circumstances or rich friends, or large capital, that create the golden opportunities of life. It is something in the person that thinks and gets an idea, and seizes the first possible moment to do what he can toward developing it.

A wise man is a maker of opportunities

To have failed once is not so much a pity as to not try again.

All business grow by what they have given to them to feed them.

To think hard and quickly, see the core of a subject, seize it and base action upon it, is the secret of successfulness.

No man's work is done on earth, so long as he can patiently labor and give anything to his family, city and nation which will add to its knowledge, wealth, improvements and importance.

Our responsibilities are making our opportunities.

All the gates of the business world are open to every one.

Business capital is good common-sense, intelligence, industry and saved-up money.

No man on earth is so happy as the man who loves his work and goes home at night with a contented heart because of a good day's work well done.

The man who makes decisions with a fixed purpose of carrying them out is, humanly speaking, unconquerable.

No honest person is down so far that he needs to stay there, unless satisfied and content with his condition.

All men may seek the great ends of wealth, honor, praise and love, but the price is high.

To believe you cannot do a thing is a way to make it impossible.

Knowledge and experience are the best two feet any one can have to equip him for successful living.

Three-quarters of all work is drudgery, unless we love it and keep cheerful.

Only an honest soul can conduct an honest business.

Every man is at his best when he adds enthusiasm to whatever he honestly believes in. Both power and progress will then enter into his undertakings.

Labor of some kind is a necessity for well-being to every human being.

No one ever did anything worth while in this world, that he was not criticized by somebody.

Happy is the man who knows he was born to work, who knows he can work, and that by work well done he can keep on climbing as other men have done, to more enjoyable and profitable work.

There are endless resources to every true man who is determined to overcome his mistakes.

Responsibilities gravitate toward persons who know most.

That which cost a lifetime to obtain may be lost in half an hour.

Time is money, with a big IS.

To almost every man known to the writer was given an elective opportunity to make or lose his way.

Many persons have an idea that one cannot be in business and lead and upright life, whereas the truth is that no one succeeds in business to any great extent, who misleads and misrepresents.

To have the disappointment of a door shut in front of us is something, but not everything. Many a time, to be stopped and forced to take another road has turned out to one's great advantage.

Money is only metal, if mentality is not back of it.

Splendid lighthouses of life are they which have been built upon the shores of obscurity by the boys of humble birth.

Success and wealth often put people to sleep, whereas they should quicken their diligence.

Failures are not fatal unless we go to sleep with them. Edison, Marconi, Cyrus W. Field, Abraham Lincoln, Ulysses S. Grant, had their failures, but each of them kept undaunted until he "won out."

There are no locks on the doors of wisdom, knowledge, honest enterprise and opportunity.

I have always had a broom in my hand.

No human being can create a great thing suddenly.

Progress is the result of self-development.

Nothing comes by merely thinking about it.

It is not possible for any man to have all the good ideas.

We must remember that the very best of us have made many mistakes.

Competition will pound us hard, but let us see who can pound hardest.

Through all these years I have just kept my heart close to the heart of the business.

The strength of men and stores and government must be in adherence to principles.

The thinking man who is true to his duty hour by hour is the man for whom there is always a place.

We shall improve every day and go ahead.

We build strong and true from the bottom up.

There is always ample room for all who do their work well.

We would rather not make a sale than make one for the buyer to regret.

A little more effort on the part of everybody to make the times better, and better times will surely come along.

I would not have been prepared to build this large store when I did, if I had not saved two and a half million dollars little by little.

Life will not be unfair with us; for duties well done there are songs along the way.

There are thousands who fall just a little short of great success by small carelessness and forgetfulness.

No business organization can rise higher than its leader and owner, constantly in the field, directing each day's plans and work. Proxies are not responsible or equal to it.

"The sleep of the laboring man is sweet" because with an honest heart he has done a good day's work.

Thoroughly great men are only men, but they do thoroughly what they do, whether it be small or great things.

Whoever lives a life of nothingness, even with wealth, or without it, is to be pitied. Just a real, fine harvest you can carry home out of the summer of your life, or no harvest at all, as you determine yourself.

To love to work and have fifty years in houses, railroad bonds, and the like; it is in himself.

What's the use of a plan if we do not work it?

They shall grow who believe they can.

It is good to have a systematic way of doing things, but it is more important to be sure that you do them.

Every man may find some good kind of opportunity in front of him if he is in earnest to avail himself of it.

It is best for a man to grow where he is planted.

Trying to fool the people is only misleading yourself.

Learn to tell the difference between activity and work.

We can find a dozen excuses: what we want is a better way.

It is easier to sell goods that are going up than goods that are going down.

A man who believes he can stand still on any height he may have risen to, doesn't understand the situation.

The best start for a good day's work is to be up and at it with the first hours of the morning.

This business was not a gift or an inheritance from rich ancestors. Its early days were days of little money, large ambitions, loads of ideas, and untiring work. The whole story is told in two words, Ambition and Work. Necessity was the teacher, and Labor was the discipline whereby we learned our lessons and prospered.

Confidence! Confidence! Confidence! That is your capital.

We have too many faults to be boastful.

It is a rare gift to know how to spend money to the best advantage.

Yesterday's best will not be accepted for to-day.

I like to stand on my feet; it makes me lazy to sit down.

Everything that is done well is hard work.

Success we get without God doesn't count up very much.

The healthiest and happiest people in the world are those privileged to work a full business day.

Wealth can no more be created safely, and permanently held, by the mere shuffling of securities, than character can be created by shuffling cards.

No man can go to prosperity over the Bridge of Business without paying a toll coin stamped Truth and Probity, and being a genuinely hard and thorough worker.

The one thousand and sixty-nine vocations in which men and women engage are one thousand and sixty-nine royal roads to greatness.

Every man and woman are capable of making a discovery that may be important and useful to the world.

Each new achievement is but a point to encamp at for one night only—the next morning to wake early and climb.

Keep up the old standards, and day by day raise them higher.

I think we have tried to do our best, but the best is yet to come.

Mr. Edison says idleness is sickness: what does he

know about it? He never indulged in it.

To get anywhere worth while, one must take a ticket of preparation, and get on the tracks of heart-effort and hammer and tongs, thick and thin endeavor.

Ideas and ideals really become the foundation of the main track of life.

You can never ride on the wave that came in and went out yesterday.

A good business should be organized in such a way that it can be independent of any man in it.

Overcome a hard job, overcome a difficult and discouraging job; fight, fight, fight, never stop!

CHARACTER BUILDING

Few lives go far without some kind of hard battle.

I cannot hold other people's tongues, and it has taken me a long time to get control of my own tongue. But it can be done, and it is well worth while. If for no other reason, it saves a lot of time!

To every man there comes a day when he must separate himself from others and act alone.

It is better to wear patched shoes and pay as you go, than to be in debt, wearing patent leathers and silken gowns.

You mend your automobile on the spot when something breaks. Don't let your life be going on with something crippled in it.

Adversity is not the worst thing that can happen to us.

Even adversity and accident are often the best bath a lazy man can fall into to wake him up to use his dormant powers. Idleness is in the main a daily drizzle of discontent and unhealthiness.

Pack your troubles in the smallest bag you have.

When any of us pass beyond the bounds of moderation in the conduct of our affairs, somebody will be hurt.

That man who forms a purpose which he knows to be right, and then moves forward to accomplish it without inquiring where it will land him as an individual, and without caring what the immediate consequences to himself will be, is the manliest of manly men.

There is no greater deception than self-deception.

No one has a right to rob his son or daughter of a noble and virtuous example.

When a man dislikes what he has made of himself, who but himself can make the changes necessary to rebuild what is unsatisfactory and displeasing? He does not need to talk about it, and no one but himself can do the job.

The finest thing in the world is to know how to belong to oneself, and not to be tossed about by the winds, doctrines and half-baked opinions which are in the air.

Almost every person has something to do which he neglects. To break one's self of that habit, simple and small as it may be, might be the turning-point to success.

To prefer death to dishonor is a finer thing than life. The man who can stand to his convictions is great in any age.

A man is not doing much until the cause he works for possesses all there is of him.

A great man is not tied to his own opinions, his hates, his preferences, or his prejudices, but is big enough to weight existing circumstances and passing events.

The man who does not learn to give early in life is generally stingy to the end.

It is a poor oversight to leave God out of our calculations.

No man can dream character into himself. He must hammer and forge himself into a man.

Everyone honors the man who fulfills a duty at all hazards.

The worse kind of lying is making promises that you cannot fulfill.

Be happy with what you have, and better things will come along.

Almost every path leads straight ahead to a worthy goal, and the heart that beats high with courage is sure to win.

Stop looking through a keyhole and come out and look at the sky.

HUMAN RELATIONS

School yourself not to keep up an argument just because you are sure you are right.

Gratitude takes three forms: a feeling in the heart, an expression in words, and a giving in return.

In a long life, so far as memory serves, the writer never saw any person, woman or man, that he did not see something beautiful in.

The more we give happiness, the more we have left.

Some people, without knowing it, carry with them a magnifying glass, with which they see, when they wish, other people's imperfections.

Have you ever noticed that the straightest stick is crooked in the water? In forming judgments of others, or in passing opinions upon current topics, let us go slow and be careful until we know all the existing circumstances.

The burdens of life become heavier whenever we fail to recognize that each of us is human, with a personality of his own.

No one was ever bankrupted by benevolence.

While we may not be able to make life a Garden of Eden, we must avoid helping to make it a Dead Sea.

The speech a man or woman makes when mad does more harm than good. Anger is always a bad speechmaker.

The whole world will serve you if you will prove that you are honestly trying to be of service to it.

Some of us may not be able to sing a note, but there is none who cannot set some other's heart a-singing!

To select your friends, companions and employees carefully, and trust them, is the best thing to do, as long experience teaches.

Few of us understand each other. Little some people know how dependent we are on something outside of ourselves. Often a single word or look would have changed an entire day. So many of us stand before each other only as closed books—contents unknown.

I do not believe in discouraging people.

I can forgive a man who does me wrong, But not until he makes the utmost restitution possible.

If there is something wrong and it is my fault, you owe it to me to come and tell me; and if it is your fault, you owe it to yourself to come and tell me.

I cannot but think that it must be a blessed thing to minister to the dying.

A man may be a fine library in himself. What does it come to if he keeps all his poetry and knowledge to himself?

It is something to be thankful for to be born with a genial spirit and gracious manners.

Just a little gift, costing one dollar, may give a thousand dollars' worth of pleasure, and be a lifelong grateful memory.

Almost everyone needs something we can give. Perhaps it is only a word, a look, a touch, a letter, or a sign of sympathy.

A man may love his business, but he needs more love than that in his life.

Isn't it only little-minded people who fail or forget to show simple courtesy?

For every courtesy, little or big, let us say, "Thank you!" to one another.

How far a cheerful look and word go in the make-up of the day's contentments!

Courtesy is a coin that we can never have too much of nor ever be stingy with.

CITIZENSHIP

Every year there's a man wanted somewhere in the United States for leadership.

We are all living under the Stars and Stripes. It is the flag of the land of our birth or the land of our adoption. We owe allegiance to no other flag.

It is not buildings or famous ancestry that make a city. It is the living men who have visions and work unselfishly to make them materialize.

There is a living Washington, a living Franklin, a living Lincoln, and a living Liberty Bell, that should always be an inspiration to us.

The country has given us everything we have got.

The people will never grumble at taxes for improvements if they can be sure they are getting full worth of the money so taken.

It is only a small shrimp of a man who does not realize that to work for the public good in some form or other is the plain duty of every citizen.

EDUCATION

There is no one whose horizon will not be widened, if he will only avail himself of the wholesome education of fellowship.

True greatness is well shown in school-teachers, never impatient, never too wearied to miss the least chance to pave the way for a little child out of his perplexities and lead him out to a hill-top.

To "loaf" on any job or avoid any plain duty is slackerism. A mother or father too busy to train a son or daughter in honor, honesty and straightforwardness is likely to regret it as a serious mistake.

Have a good book to read all the time.

I will not stand still: I must learn all the time.

Wisdom can be learned from living examples better than from books which, in the main, speak only to our eyes.

To wise people it is given to be in school everyday, learning something interesting and useful from every incident of life.

To waste time with people from whom we can learn nothing is a losing business.

Idle men think they know enough.

The greatest need of this present-day world is more smilers, singers, patient, good-natured, strong-minded men and women. Teachers, train the children so to be.

The Sunday-school, wherever it has had proper development, comes nearer than any other religious agency to answering the greater needs of the human race.

Poetry is a great teacher, whether it be in words, or music, or other expression of great thoughts.

I have lost time, strength, money in every direction, but never anything that was spent upon a Sunday-school.

It is not good enough to be well read. We must help others by what we read.

Knowledge is not power unless there is forehanded-ness to keep the tank full of gasoline and have on board a supply of the right make of rubber tires, as well as the tinkering things for a broken-down engine or springs.

Selected Prayers of
JOHN WANAMAKER

Publisher's Dedication

to

DR. BEN KAIN
Who faithfully read one of the Wanamaker prayers at a weekly Bible study

THE MAKING OF A
"Merchant Prince"
Notes and Prayers of his Mother

****

My whole soul whispers God bless you. The sweet incense of your dear faithful love followed me through the night and now goes on with the day. Mother

****

The care and thought you have given your old and young Mother have been marvelous. How could I inspire such affection in a boy? So undeserving. If the game of tenth were played, you would have ten to, your credit every time and I not one!   Mother

****

Happy is the Mother who can rest content that her Boy has learned the things which belong to His Peace. 1910

****

I kiss you a thousand times, as deeply and fondly as I love you. I find my joy and happiness in being loved by you today, my dear precious Boy. February-13th, 1905.

****

I am praying day and night for your guardian angels to watch and guide more closely and bring the Divine Peace that is yours. Your dear Mother - 1918

INTRODUCTION

No one ever attending Bethany Sunday School, in the sixty-five years when Mr. Wanamaker was the active superintendent, could fail to be impressed by his prayers from the desk. Those contained in this volume are but a few of the ones preserved in his own handwriting.

There can be no doubt of his unfaltering faith in the power of prayer. He was a man of prayer, and to him the unseen world was not only real but constantly near. The following sentence in his writing expresses the experience of his own life:

When men learn to pray they shorten the distance between earth & heaven

Because he was a man of prayer he was an humble man. Memory brings back the picture of a man who was childlike in the simplicity of his life and faith. A little child was unawed in his presence, and the humblest of men could approach him and feel at ease.

From his prayer life came also his life of deep meditation. Our day seems to have lost, to a large measure, the spirit and practice of meditation. But not so with Mr. Wanamaker. Many an hour was given up to meditation upon the mysteries of the spiritual life and the world of nature round about. His prayers throb with originality and uniqueness, even as did all his life, which were born in the quiet times of meditation. Every bird in the springtime, the greening lawns and fields, the blossoming trees, as also the starry heavens, had their message for his listening ears tuned to catch their beauty by the hours of meditation.

And out of this prayerful meditation came the life of lofty aspiration which was his. His prayers are marked with a dissatisfaction with present attainments and a constant reaching out to the heights of future exaltation and accomplishment. Surely of his life too might it be written: "Forgetting the things that were behind, he pressed forward unto those things that were before."

> *"More things are wrought by prayer*
> *Than this world dreams of."*

A. GORDON MACLENNAN

Bethany Church,
Philadelphia, Pa.

O GOD, we cannot mistake Thy presence in the world; help us to recognize Thy voice in the mighty wind from Thy hand upon the sea, and in the great flood wherewith Thou dost imperil a city. Thou dost say to man, "Thou mayest navigate the air by thy skill, and thou mayest extract the electric mystery from the sky, but in an hour, to-night or tomorrow, the cities may cave in, and the streets may have boats of hungry in them looking for bread. From all corners of earth, be still, and know that I am God."

Turn us back to-day to the Book Thou hast written for us. Give us enlightenment of mind. Let blessing come like great wave from heaven. Let Thy voice fill the heaving of our souls; bring us into inner chambers and lift us up with new and immortal hope.

We confess our sins and mourn our iniquity. Bring us all around the Cross and Thou blessed Son of God, our only Priest and Saviour, show us that Thy forgiveness is greater than our guilt. Amen.

MERCIFUL FATHER, by Thy grace we again have access to Thy Throne. We thank Thee that we have seen Thy face and that we have heard the music of Thy voice. We have had revealed to us the gentleness of Thy Fatherliness through the life of Thy Son. We humble ourselves before Thee and pray that the law and life that Thy Son expounded and exampled may displace our low, small, cunning lives, as the summer sun meets the snow and causes it to melt and the earth to bring forth an abounding harvest. Some of us are still in the winter-time of our lives. O Thou, who created the earth and dost recreate in the passing seasons, work upon our stony hearts and reclothe us with the beauty of a redeeming and spiritual nature.

We supplicate Thee, O Father and King, at this moment for a new manhood through the enabling Christ, whose yoke is easy and whose burden is light. Amen.

"There are many who choose to live underground, whose minds are lighted only by prejudices and jealousies. They see nothing clearly, and wonder why."

MOST MERCIFUL FATHER, Thou callest us to Thee, and Thou wilt come to us in Thine own way. We shall know Thy coming by the warmth of our hearts, by the obedience of our spirits and by our willingness to renounce ourselves and receive Thyself.

We are travelling a road that often distresses us by its length and roughness. Draw near to join us, and expound the Scriptures that we may forget our tiredness. Come through the door and sit with us; make our hearts to know Thee by dissatisfaction with old ways, old appetites and by horror of evil words and deeds. Pity us in the weakness of the flesh; help us in the struggle and make us victors. Let us not lie wounded in the wilderness of the wanderers to bleed to death in remorse on beds of thorns and pain. Turn our faces toward the gates of light, and swing back the doors of the kingdom, gentle Jesus. Let this be the hour of the power of Thy grace, Thou redeeming, healing Jesus. Amen.

"It is poor prosperity that is blind to the need of God's favor."

O GRACIOUS SAVIOUR, when we sat in the darkness of our sins Thou didst come to us to shed light on our way. Often when bowed down in distress and dark times Thou didst comfort us. In this holy hour, draw near, and make our communion sweet and profitable.

Blessed one, Life of life, and Light of light, lift any shadow on our hearts and let the clear shining of Thy face be manifest. Draw out to Thyself our tenderest affections and over and against each heart may the sign of the Cross plainly reveal to us the love of the suffering, dying Saviour. While we talk of Him who was once crucified, now the risen Lord, draw near to be transfigured. Illumine our lives that they may be one continual day. As Thou dost pour light from Thy heavens on the hilltop and on the lowly vale, on the great trees and the smallest plants and flowers and out on the broad gray sea, so bless every man and satisfy every hungry soul by the richness of Thy provisions. Amen.

"The richer some men grow, the smaller they seem."

O SUN OF RIGHTEOUSNESS, mystery of light, may we shed forth Thy brightness, that others may see and be blest. Enable us to abandon all of darkness and so to walk that others following us may not stumble.

Give us eager desires for more light. Make us good listeners. Forbid that the music of heaven should die on our ears. Let it find its way into our souls and redouble itself that we may read Thy Word eagerly, diligently, pryingly, persistently; and letting no message escape us. Teach us that gratitude and praise promote larger gifts. God be merciful and gracious.

O Mighty Prince and Saviour, Son of God, Lamb of God, Only Begotten of the Father, we cling to Thy mercy seat, not knowing what else to do, crying, "Forgive our sins, and make us fruitful in all good works." Encompass our souls that we may be living temples by reason of the ministry of the Eternal Spirit. Amen.

"Life's little things are most potential for our happiness."

O LORD, not far from any of us, and we believe Thou art very near. In our early mornings together Thou hast told us to ask and it shall be given us, to knock and it shall be opened unto us, to seek and we shall find.

We know that those who do not ask deserve to go without. Surely we cannot hope to find if we do not seek, and it is lamentable to let the gate of heaven be shut if we refuse to knock, forget to knock, when no one knocks in vain.

For everyone that asketh receiveth, and he that seeketh findeth, and to him who knocketh it shall be opened. Not words, but acts; Not the man that says he will, but he that doth. We know the winds must blow; the rains must descend and the floods fall, but may we get on solid foundation, that we may be with those of whom it shall be said, "It fell not, for it was founded upon the Rock."

May we be in the spirit of worship on the Lord's Day. Thou hast done great things. We bless Thee for goodness and love. Amen.

"A silent hour with happy thoughts is a restorative without a doctor's prescription."

LIVING AND LOVING GOD, God of life and God of love, we worship Thee as our heart's only God. We are sinners. God be merciful unto us. We have had a festival of hunger and a dance of shame. We have had spasms of consciousness and went straight on in willful, stubborn, disobedience. We tried to drown them in liquor and wrong doing, but we are determined not to play the devil's game any longer.

We come in through the door of unworthiness and the door of helplessness. We see a nail-scarred Hand reaching down to us, and a little ladder marked Faith. We pull ourselves together and place our sore and unfit feet upon it to climb to the Hospital of Mercy, to put our case in the Friendly Physician's hands.

Eternal Father so pitiful; Eternal Christ so tender; Eternal Spirit so patient; heal and help and hold on to us with mighty love, full pardon, and abounding grace. Amen.

"It is not the length of life that counts. It is its depth and purpose."

OUR LOVING FATHER, we are here, to-day, resting in Thy goodness. Wilt Thou unloose our tongues to praise Thee? With invisible hands Thou dost take away our days and we know not how many remain. We commence a new month and almost one half of this year is behind us. So teach us to number our days that we may apply our hearts unto wisdom. We have caught at the baits upon the devil's hooks and everything was bitterness and ashes, and there is a great crying pain in our hearts for our blindness and our folly, and we come back ragged and dirty as the Prodigal came.

Scorn us not for our weakness and humiliations and open the door that we may come in to Thee and fall at Thy feet confessing our waywardness and wanderings. Lord, heal the disease of sin, and may we live no longer in the buffeting of the wind, but be forgiven and at home, in the Father's house. Amen.

"There are ninety-and-nine blessings, in most lives, to one misfortune, where good health, intelligence, integrity, commonsense and energy exist."

O GOD, we join in the song of praise for this new day, so light and bright. We thank Thee for its welcome to God's house and we receive it as a token of Thy mercies, that Thou wilt send upon us according as our faith triumphs over doubt. Thou dost distribute Thy gifts variously, but Thou knowest where the gifts are, and Thou wilt ask an account of the mechanic that makes the automobile, and the laborer who cleans it. Blessed is that servant, who, when his Lord cometh, shall be found waiting, watching and ready.

Lift the deep shadows of war that make the earth seem like a yawning grave, with death on the right hand and a great fear and misery on the left. God bless the President, and every man that looks for a way to complete the task that is ours. Thou art the King of kings and Lord of lords and all thrones are under Thy feet. O Prince of Peace, take the sceptre of government and rule. Amen.

"Time is old, but every new morning is young. It comes to us saying, "Her I am to help you; use me well."

ALMIGHTY GOD, this great universe that Thou hast created by Thy power carries Thy smile and testifies to us Thy presence in this holy place which bears Thy Name. If a building on earth be regarded as sacred to the memory of Lincoln or Grant or the Declaration of Independence, much more is this great earth sacred as the temple of Thy making! Teach us that there is no unholy ground, since Thy Son, Jesus Christ, has been here, and His footprints and His grave have blessed it all.

Oh, the depth of the richness of Thy love. In this love we stand, and live, and are saved. We praise Thee that Thou didst purchase us, who being slaves to sin and on our way to the prison-house of Death, didst buy us, not with silver or gold, but with the precious blood of a Lamb without blemish, and without spot, even the blood of the Christ. Amen.

"Man is the only creature on the globe that ignores the Creator and defies His right to arrange the harmonies of His own world for the happiness of its people."

O LORD, Thou openest Thine hand and satisfiest the desire of every living creature. Yet with all Thy manifold goodnesses, man is a mean guest at Thy table. He comes only with half of himself,—with his legs and his hands, but only a mite of his heart and his head. We misjudge our Father, and are led away by foolish counsels and silly prejudices. The littleness and blindness and narrowness of us turn our hearts into silent chambers, never open to the God who made us. We confess that it seems as if we had read in our Bibles that God spent most of His time asleep, instead of that His eyes are upon all.

Help us to see the ditches and pits we are digging for eternal years with our own hands. Let none of us hear when the night is dark and the stars have set, "Depart from me, ye cursed." We plead Thy mercy through our Lord Jesus Christ. Amen.

"Life is a beautiful thing. Our Heavenly Father did not put us down here to mourn and lose ourselves in some kind of fog."

OUR FATHER, we look along the road Thou hast brought us. On left hand and right are Thy stores of remembrance and mercy. Thou hast not forgotten us, though the road be crowded, and we say, "Praise the Lord who hath helped us." Do Thou stay by. Prevent us from standing still or sitting down. Help us to fight the good fight and to endure to the end; to be among those who overcome. Help us to live on the Word of Christ—the blood and strength of souls. Hear us, Saviour and Holy Spirit, for we are praying at the all-saving Cross. Thy miracles are in our health, peace, companionship. Look upon those only half-turned homeward. Teach them another step today, and may they go on and be found quite at home by the sun-setting. Let a great joy, liberty and confidence seize our hearts. When our short day on earth is done, may we find it to be no day at all but a brief night before an infinite morning. Amen.

"Where did the birds go to school to learn how to build nests?"

WHEN I consider thy heavens, O God, and the work of thy hands, what is man that thou art mindful of him, and the son of man that thou visitest him?" The heavens are telling Thy glory and all Thy works do praise Thee. Thou waterest the hills and dost make the valleys laugh with corn. Thou dost give food to man and beast, so that none lack or suffer hunger. We hail Thee as the maker of Heaven and earth. Thou wilt not forsake the work of Thy hands, but wilt bring it all to completion.

We thank Thee for the religious instinct and the strange mysterious hunger of our hearts. "As the hart panteth after the water brooks, so panteth my soul after thee, O God." We come to bless Thee for this Thy day of rest, for this Thy house of peace, and Thy Book of revelation. We bring our sins to be forgiven, Lord. Send some strong angel to smite the foe of our souls, and bring us, we beseech Thee, to victory. Amen.

"God hears a woman's prayers, I believe, before He hears any other."

FATHER ALMIGHTY, the one God of power and love, the world Thou hast made and dost keep, illustrates Thy goodness. No human being could make the sky so blue and light it with millions upon millions of heaven-made candles. All earth-made candles flicker out, but for unnumbered years Thou hast sent us messages of light and love in the sunbeams of the day and from the distant stars in the night. Already the soft air bears us, from the southern fields and gardens and grassy plains, the gospel of fragrance, of might and of grace. We love to think of Thee as the God of the woods, green meadows and cornfields. Let us not lose the power to spell Thy Name in the grass, the leaves and the sunlit sky.

Thou dost make the winter days short for us and the summer days long. Help us to see Thee in all life's processes, to keep company with fresh-air people, and to never be far from Thy Son whose Cross was cut out of the woods and who slept in the grave in the garden and walked like a gardener in the morning. Lead us to Him to say "Rabboni!"

WE thank Thee, our Father, for Thy Word—the eternal music which comes into our hearts and brings us to faith and love and prayer.

We bless Thee for Thy care. We cannot tell where it begins and it never ends. It opens the way to the heavens. Though we are always dying, yet we cannot die, even though our flesh must fall into the grave. Death is the porch of immortality given to us by our Lord Jesus Christ, and by His power our spirits shall rise to praise Him through endless years. Give us patience to wait and do His will; give us the deep rest of faith, a sweet and tender repose in God. Teach us the mission and power of discipline.

Turn our hair white with age; break down our backs; take the roof from over our heads, but take not Thy Holy Spirit from us. Teach us the meekness and charity of Christ, in whose Name we pray. Amen.

"Pride is a dangerous taskmaster"

OUR FATHER, Thou hast given us fifty-two blessed Sundays in the year to be shining lamps to brighten our way. We have studied together, chapter after chapter, for years and years, but we have not finished school. We cannot lay down the Book of God, which constantly throws new light on the Father and the world to come.

Thou didst also speak a word to us out of the daybreak of the wintry sky when Thou didst show us that it is possible for Thee to break through the cold and darkness of December and pour a flood of golden light over the snow. And Thou didst show us that, when all the years have fled, there will be a daybreak over our graves; that the graves will be but a resurrection cradle, and that we shall be forever with the Lord. Make us to know the power of our Lord's Resurrection for Thy glory. Amen.

"God never made a man just because He wanted one more man: He wanted you. He started you with a different-shaped head, different face, and different thoughts."

O GOD, our God, we come to Thee in the Name of Jesus, for without His Name there is no prayer. He is our sufficiency and in His sufficiency we abound. He is our propitiation and great High Priest. We live not by our own strength but lean upon the arm Almighty, resting upon the heart all tender, comforted by the love never failing.

O God, we have heard of the sting of Death, but we have heard also of Christ the Victor, the bright and morning Star. We take the pierced Hand and trust to the blood that flowed from His side. We thank Thee that it is an infinite election and yet Thou dost whisper to us to "take heed lest thou fall, or slip, or be thrown down." Our Father, we will not trifle with Thy love, but pray that we, by Thy grace, may walk in the light as He is in the light, and the glory shall all be Thine. Amen.

"We do well to hark back for light and inspiration to our great men's clear visions, sturdy purposes and safe examples."

OUR FATHER, we come into Thy garden to gather flowers of hope, of recovery and joy. We bless Thee that Thou hast called us to rejoice, and we will, if Thou wilt lift upon us the shining of Thy countenance. We bless Thee for these four walls that form this house of security and calm and peace. Give us the stillness of faith and certainty of triumph.

From the very beginning Thou hast declared Thyself a God of love. But also Thou hast revealed Thyself as a hater of sin, but all through Thou hast been pitiful and forgiving. We thank Thee that finally, "even as Moses lifted up the serpent in the wilderness, so the Son of Man must be lifted up." Lord, we thank Thee, to-day, as a nation and a family for that lifting up and pray Thee to bring us all at last to the blessed, new, immortal life. Come nearer and nearer to us until the rests of these summer days shall lengthen into the summer of Heaven's eternal rest. Amen.

"It is a tremendous thing to live. dying is next to nothing."

WE remember, Lord, that while John was preaching by Jordan a humble, silent, industrious Man at Nazareth was working at the carpenter's bench. But the day that closed the door of that carpenter's shop was when the Man went to the synagogue and opened the Scriptures and read, "The Spirit of the Lord is upon me because he hath anointed me to preach the gospel to the poor; he hath sent me to heal the broken hearted, to preach deliverance to the captives, and recovering of sight to the blind, to set at liberty them that are bruised, to preach the acceptable year of the Lord;" and He added, "This day is this Scripture fulfilled in your ears." We thank Thee that John heard and saw and said, "Behold the Lamb of God, which taketh away the sin of the world." We thank Thee for the voice out of the sky at Jordan— "This is my beloved Son: hear him." May we begin to prepare the way of the Lord in our lives and by our service. In His Name, we pray. Amen.

"Truth can always stand up by herself."

WE are glad, our Father, that we did not live in the time when none could approach Thee except by priests and Levites, and in a time, ages ago, when the high priests could not approach Thee within the veil but once a year. It is permitted to us, at all times, every day and hour, to approach Thee through Thy Son, Thy offered and, by us, accepted Saviour. We thank Thee that by His precious blood we are redeemed; we thank Thee for the Spirit of God, whereby the love of God the Father is shed abroad in our hearts and we thank Thee that the Spirit talks of the things of Christ and shows them unto us so that we may be brought into the glorious liberty of the children of God.

We thank Thee, blessed Holy Ghost, that Thou didst ever bring us into a state of holy fellowship with the Father and the Son. We pray Thee, this day, to especially elevate and sanctify us that we may be filled with a joyful expectation of dwelling, now and to all eternity, in the immediate presence of Him whom though unseen we love, arid in whom we rejoice with joy unspeakable. Amen.

O LORD, we thank Thee that Thou dost permit us to speak to Thee in prayer, to tell our thoughts and express our desires. We believe that Thou wilt do what is right and best for us, not to our poor seeing, perhaps, but best in the end, when Thou dost bring in the revealing morning to tell the secrets of time.

Thou knowest our littleness and peevishness; count them not against us. Stoop to our weakness and grant us a long hearing. We leave everything with Thee, the God of beginning; we leave it with Thee, O Christ, the Gethsemane sufferer; we leave it with Thee, O Holy Ghost, who broodest over man to help him.

We are all prodigals, having gone far afield, but now behold us returning, confessing our sin and shame. We have sinned personally against Thee, and personally seek Thy forgiveness. Great redeeming Son of God, pity us poor sinners and show us Thy grace. Amen.

"Let those who follow me continue to build with the plumb of Honor, the level of Truth and the square of Integrity, Education, Courtesy and Mutuality."

GRACIOUS and unforgetting Father, Thou hast brought us out of sick rooms and hospitals and homes, that have been sheltered from storms and ills, in great mercy by Thy tender care to the beginning of another month. We have been a long time journeying together— some of us about fifty years— still we gather about the Altar of the Cross and thank the God and Father of our Lord for the Incarnation and for redemption through His Son—He who became a Man—a mystery beyond fathoming; He redeemed man, love beyond words, thoughts or dreams. Yet we enter into it as we do into the mystery of the sky with its light and beauty, its springs and summers yet unborn. We have been unworthy of Thy bountiful love. We have grieved Thee; God be merciful to such sinners and their trouble. Thou hast had to try us with tormenting cares, severe afflictions. Yet in many ways Thou hast shown great love. May we in some degrees show ardour, love and faith. May we kiss the guardian Hand who meets us with love and not with clubs. Amen.

"Only poverty and idleness embitter life."

WE do not always understand Thy care, our Father, but Thy great hand of love always covers us. This is enough, and we stand up to do our part the best we can. Show us Thy signature, now and then, that we may know that we are on the right road. For Thy Book we bless Thee. It is like none other. Our heart answers to it as to none other. We are eternity-bound. Good Shepherd, accompany us homeward. Divine Teacher, hold the lamp to our feet. Thou of the Cross, speak to us that we may find the way to Paradise. Thy Church is the light in earth's dark place. In our guilt and helplessness Thou art our refuge. The sweetest of all music is the blessed Gospel of the Son of Man come to seek and to save. As we think of it the tears dry in our eyes, the aching stops in our hearts and infinite peace fills our being. Pity us, who are poor children of the dust. Blessed Lord of the poor and the tired, help us to hold on to the plough until the going down of the sun. This is our prayer in Jesus' Name. Amen.

"The man of all men I am most afraid of is myself."

O LORD, our God, Thou hast taught us to make supplications and intercession, and to whom we are directed to give thanks, we beseech Thee to receive our prayers offered to Thy Divine Majesty. We thank Thee that Thou hast unveiled Thyself and made known to us Thy attributes of love, mercy, justice and power. Thou hast given us a revelation of Thyself in Thy Holy Word, which came in old time, not by the will of man, but by holy men who spake as they were moved by the Holy Ghost. We bless Thee that Thou hast crowned Thy revelation in Jesus Christ, who was made in the likeness of sinful man. We praise Thee for His wondrous grace, large-thoughted care, patient endurance, calm self-denial and sacrifice, even down to the dark hour of Calvary.

O blessed Christ, Thy finished work on earth in purchasing salvation is over. Come back again and walk with us, who must toil and suffer in the fulfillment of life's task, that we may exemplify the truths and hope of Thy Gospel in daily service. We ask this in Thy precious Name. Amen.

ALMIGHTY GOD, we said we would come to worship Thee in common fellowship. We are glad to be of one mind, and in Thy house. We thank Thee for the Lord's Day and house, and for the Saviour and for the Holy Ghost. May this place be as a mountain-top, with the clouds all below it.

May we feel here the soft, balmy winds of heaven and be refreshed. We thank Thee for the teaching of our Lord Jesus Christ, in whose Name and by whose grace we have an open way to the foot of the Throne. We know that our sins are great, but we also know that Thy grace is greater than our sins, because Thy voice has spoken tenderly, plainly and pleadingly.

Thou makest all things new. We pray for a deeper manhood; a redeemed nature that we may be ripening in the Sun of righteousness. Interpret to us Thy Word to-day, and thereby clothe us with strength and adorn us with beauty. Amen.

"Corn and men have to be ripened and well seasoned to be of any good."

ON THIS HALLOWED GROUND OF GETTYSBURG, CONSECRATED BY ABRAHAM LINCOLN, THE MARTYRED PRESIDENT, TODAY, AFTER THE LAPSE OF HALF A CENTURY, THE NORTH AND SOUTH MEET WITH THE EAST AND WEST, UNDER THE NATION'S FLAG, TO DO HONOR TO THE SOLDIERS STILL LIVING AND TO PAY LOVING AND RESPECTFUL HOMAGE TO THOSE WHO ARE ASLEEP IN THE STILLEST OF ALL SLUMBERS. NEITHER STRESS OF TIME NOR DISTANCE OF HOME SHALL BREAK OR BLUR THE FRIENDSHIPS OUR BROTHERS SEALED WITH THEIR OWN BLOOD. THE WHITE STONES OF MEMORIAL ERECTED BY GRATEFUL COMRADES, TO MARK THE DEEDS OF VALOR ACCOMPLISHED HERE, ALSO INSPIRE TO DUTY AND HIGH ENDEAVOR THE EFFORTS OF ALL GENERATIONS. IN THIS CATHEDRAL OF THE LIVING AND THE DEAD, WE PAUSE AT THE CLOSE OF DAY, HANDS CLASPING HANDS, HEADS AND HEARTS IN SILENCE, BOWING, TO SAY A PRAYER FOR EACH OTHER AND OUR BELOVED COUNTRY, THAT PEACE AND FRATERNITY MAY ABIDE UNTIL THE TRUMP SHALL SOUND AND LIFE'S SHADOWS FLEE AWAY FOREVER.